l

in a

silver mist

pictures and words inspired by the
landscape of the south west of
england

Paul newman

j a harris &

paul newman

DEDICATION

For our grandmothers.

CONTENTS

ACKNOWLEDGMENTS

We'd like to acknowledge all our teachers.
You know who you are...

INTRODUCTION

I grew up in Sussex where I spent my summers roaming the South Downs. Often the sky would be full of butterflies over the meadows, a natural phenomena I still dream about. Those swarms of Red Admirals, Chalkhill Blues and Orange-tips just don't exist any more.

Nature is my place of refuge.

After studying Psychology at university and training as a teacher, I took the advice of an author friend and went off to Bath Spa to gain a Masters in Creative Writing.

I'm the author of countless personal poems and *The Wolf in Your Bed*', a non-fiction book about therapeutic writing. I'm currently working on a novel, a psychological thriller - 'A *Deadly*

Yearning'.

These days I make a living writing, editing and teaching creative writing.

Paul Newman's fragile, beautiful work is like a gateway to my love of the landscape and humanity's place within it. Paul's images have a quality which make me reflect on the complexity of being human and part of nature, yet somehow detached from it.

As a child my favourite artist was Albrecht Durer. An artist of great sensitivity, his careful attention to detail was like a resting place in the midst of all the chaos of growing up.

When I look at the work of Paul Newman, I get the same sense of calm and inspiration. As though his drawings are a place for me to breathe, to think, to recollect, reconnect and refine.

I wrote each poem in response to one of Paul's drawings. The pictures led me to creative reflections on the earth, war, birth, love, loss, beauty, history and the ancestors – on everything that separates us from nature, and everything that brings us closer.

In order to make this book a bit different from the exhibition of words and images held at the Old Print Room gallery in November 2014, we decided to include a short story with this collection. Also inspired by Paul's drawings of Dartmoor, it was written by Jill is called The Goddess of Haytor.

We hope you enjoy this book and take the chance to practice some deeper contemplation of your own as you examine Paul's images and read Jill's words.

With love, J & P x

1

ASH SKYWARD

LOOKING UP FROM THE SUMMIT OF LEWESDON
HILL, WINTER 2011.

wood, water, stone.

on top of hills and
mountains

all of us are - prophets

all of us -

pilgrims.

2

WRITHING ASH

A CIRCUIT ON CRANBORNE CHASE, NOVEMBER 2013.

autumn.

an ash tree by the path -

press your hand against the bark

as the hunter takes a beat.

in the distance -

    gunfire.

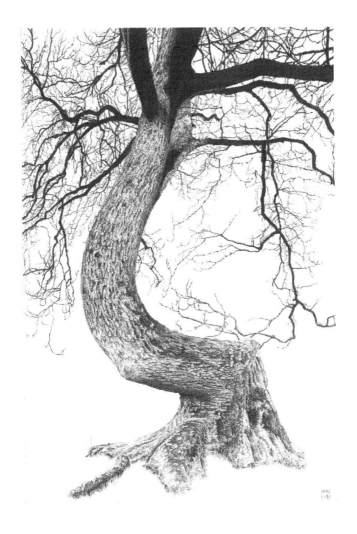

3

DAY'S END AT EGGARDON HILL

NOTES ABOVE A HILLFORT, LATE SUMMER, 2008.

twilight -

swifts fly above the shadows.

why must the day end?

4

BOULDERS BREAK THE SURFACE

STILLNESS-

"THEY BOTH LISTENED SILENTLY TO THE WATER, WHICH TO THEM WAS NOT JUST WATER, BUT THE VOICE OF LIFE, THE VOICE OF BEING, THE VOICE OF PERPETUAL BECOMING."
HERMANN HESSE, SIDDARTHA

- RIVER DART, AUTUMN 2013

at summer's height

the river.

three boulders break the surface -

listen.

5

A CONFLUENCE OF WATERS

THE WAY IT RUSHES OVER THE STONE, AUTUMN 2013.

morning.

a confluence of waters on the moor

and everything is - washed

away.

6

IMMINENT

SHIPSTAL POINT, ARNE, THE TIDE HAS RETREATED, HUNGRY WADERS MOVE IN FOR A MEAL. OVERHEAD CLOUDS ARE LOOMING. LATE SUMMER, 2007

green island, round island,

brownsea island.

clouds gather overhead.

below the water -

oil the colour

           of old blood.

                .

7

PATH TO GOLDEN CAP

SEARCHING FOR ST CATHERINE, I'M *IN* THE
HILL AND THEN THE MIST... DATE AND TIME
FORGOTTEN

winter path -

rooks calling

from high branches.

the wanderer -

drifts.

8

LIGHT DISTILLED ON LEWESDON
HILL

IT'S AUTUMN AGAIN, FINALLY I GET IT. THE
IMAGE IS CLEAR.

shadows, autumn

mist - is light

distilled.

there is water underground -

and soldiers marching

in the desert.

9

WHEN THE WOOD HEARS

beeches stand proud on their banks, but
some with shallow roots have succumbed to
early storms and lay like limbs,
straddling the nearby ditches which are
lined with copper leaves, autumn 2011.

leaves burning -

smoke rising from the valley.

a wind sings high in the branches.

beneath the tree roots -

the ancestors' bones

are whispering.

10

HAYTOR GASPING

BATHOLITH, FELDSPAR, CLITTER, HEIGHT OF
SUMMER 2009

a skylark sings.

a soldier climbs the tor and

stoops - with cupped hands –

shaking -

drinks water

from a pool of rain.

there's more to human sacrifice

than dying.

COME DOWN

11

REACHING KES TOR WELL

RESTORATION IN NATURE ARRIVES AT UNEXPECTED MOMENTS, APRIL 2009

on kes tor the moon -

reflected in a rockpool

waits for you to feel

    - that passionate shift

of mind

and the curious movement of

stone.

12

TURNED TO STONE [ALDERS, PULLABROOK BRIDGE]

LAVA TO ROCK, WOOD TO STONE, ROCK TO WATER, SPRING 2004.

summer morning – light

falls slant – footsteps echo

a traveller crosses over.

if i could build a bridge of words

between us

would i hesitate?

13

CHASE OF A SENSATION AT BELLEVER TOR

LOST IN THE MIDDLE OF THIS VASTNESS; IN THE MOOR IN THE MIST AND MY SELF.WHAT WAS I PURSUING?(MID-SUMMER 2009, BETWEEN 4 AND 9PM, LIGHT FALLING, VISIBILITY DECREASING)

in monochrome sighs -

you climb to stand on stone.

and the granite glistens after rain

at the close of day -

and the vast and liquid universe

always flowing through us.

14

BAPTISM AT MIDDLE BERE

"ALL LIFE IS BEING LIVED."

RILKE, FROM THE BOOK OF HOURS.

dusk and the nightjar's

skittering call.

a wind blowing - sets

the bog orchid trembling.

a man sinking

in water - transforming.

the goddess of haytor

Bran, son of Gerren, King of the Corn for
a single year, waited for death on top of
the High Rock. He closed his hands
around the empty cup crushing it until
it crumbled. It was a thousand breaths
since he drank the spiced tea of visions
it contained. His mouth still tasted of
the bitter herbs.

When she gave him the drink at dawn his
mother had said to him:

    'This will make it easier to bear. The
vision it gives you will bless you and
make sense of your sacrifice. In the end
you'll understand that death does not
exist at all. You'll be part of the
goddess forever as you have been since
the first birth.'

    'I'm a warrior,' he said, 'death is my
shadow. I'm not afraid of anything.'

    She sighed and ran her hands over his
upturned face. 'Ever since you were born
I knew you'd be the harvest king. You
were so strong, beautiful and healthy.
I'm sad to lose you even though you'll
always be with me.'

    A single tear ran down her cheek.

    He stood up from the pallet and went

to the doorway of the roundhouse, looking
out over the village. The birdsong of
morning surrounded him.

Never had first light seemed so
numinous and full of promise. His wife's
house lay on the far edge of the green
and he wondered if she was awake yet.

The thought that he would never see
her again, touch her soft curves or
cradle her silky head in his arms made
his heart cold. Would she weep for him?

At this time of day she'd be suckling
the babies. His twin sons. The thought
of them was like falling into a bed of
thorns so he pushed the thought away. He
had a duty to perform.

'The king must die,' he said.

His mother said softly, 'so is it
below as above in the heavens.'

'I lied,' he said, 'I'm very afraid.'

At that point a group of fifteen or so
men materialised out of the forest to the
west of the village. The hunting party
of Danu. They would chase him to the
rock and wait, shouting for him to jump,
for his body to fall so they could each
stab him with their swords and dance and
sing the blood-song.

One of the men stepped forward, his
brother Eavan, short and dark-tempered.
Eavan broke away from the group and made
his way towards Bran with his head low.
Bran greeted him and they embraced.

'I will not let you die,' Eavan
whispered.

Bran tried to pull away. 'What are you
saying brother?'

'Simply that the world is changing.'

'You know the saying,' Bran said, 'the
queen dies in birth and the king must die
in love for the earth. It's always been
so.'

Eavan put his face up close to Bran's.
His breath smelled of ale and a fierce
light burned in his eyes.

'It's time for a change,' Eavan said
and whilst he spoke he slipped something
heavy into the pouch that hung around
Bran's waist. Bran put his hand there to
feel the object. It was a knife, the
short, heavy blade excellent for close
combat. He frowned. Why had his brother
given him a deadly weapon?

The wind was soft but persistent making a
flutish sound as it entered the small
crevices and gullies of the high rock.

Bran knelt by a hollow filled with
recent rain. He dipped his finger in the
water and made the sign of fertility on
his forehead. Then he said his prayers
according to tradition.

He prayed to the goddess and her
consort, blessed his wife and children,
gave thanks for his seed and the
abundance of the past year. As the King

of the Corn he had wanted for nothing.

Memories of that past year engulfed him.

After his announcement. The twelve handmaids who served him sweet fruits, stewed roots and the best meat. They combed out his hair and washed his body with soapwort in the forest spring.

All the women of the village as they paid him homage. They worshiped him as an equal of the goddess. They brought him gifts. Woven cloaks and rugs. Clay figures of the ancestors, animal spirits and pressed herb oils. They laughed at his jokes and danced for him, sang him to sleep, kissed his face and body in homage.

The wife who chose him. Her mind as quick as the fox. Her body a reflection of the goddess in high summer.

And when the children of his wife were born and seen to be strong as him, he was allowed to give his seed to the handmaids too. The thought of their pink flesh as they parted their legs made him shudder.

Even now, even here so close to death - he felt himself respond as only a man could.

How could he leave all this behind?

A red cloud of rage entered his mind. He flexed his arms and watched the muscles grow taut. He was strong enough to seize that life back.

By the gods of war and death he could

make all women bow to him and his
brothers too.

The goddess Danu came to him just as the
sun hit its zenith in the summer sky.
His head was light as air and he was
nauseous, as if he'd drunk too much
fermented apples laced with sacred fungi.

Those bitter visionary herbs allowed
him to see the Otherworld and the goddess
who ruled there.

Her hair was as black as earth, her
eyes the colour of rivers and her lips as
red as berries. She wore an emerald gown
of the finest linen. Her hands and bare
feet were painted with orange earth dye,
swirling with patterns, sigils, leaves
and symbols of life and death.

She reached out her arms to him.

Bran stood up and bowed to her but his
heart felt nothing. She stepped towards
him and made the sign of blessing with
her fingers but he refused to open the
door of his mind to her mercy.

'What mercy do you show me?' he asked,
'if my next action is to jump to my death
for your sake?'

Danu smiled, her eyes the only part of
her face showing her age and he saw for a
moment the wisdom of time shining within
them. It should have broken him, that
look of deep intimacy with all things.
But instead it made him reach inside his
pouch and fold his hand around the blade

nestling within.

'You don't understand,' she said, her
voice as soft as the breeze, 'it isn't me
you must die for.'

'I don't have to die for anyone if I
choose not to.'

'Your brothers are hoping for a kill.
It's them you have to satisfy. Without
the ritual they'll have no boundaries.'

She shook back her hair and he noticed
how heavy her breasts were, how enticing
her nipples. He wanted to rip at her
dress and see what lay beneath. He could
smell her womanly scent and it enraged
him. The sounds of the hunting party
below drifted upwards. The men beating
their drums to make the sound of the
thunder god.

They sang the blood-song, they shouted
for the goddess to appear, they screamed
for Bran to jump onto their swords.

He wanted to go among them and join
with them in the dance. But the dance
was only performed when the sun was down
and the moon showed her face to the world
and his blood was painted on the faces of
the men, his brothers.

'What if I break the cycle?' he said,
'what if I refuse to take part in your
savagery? What then?'

'It will be worse for you and your
children and their descendants until the
end of the age,' she said and her voice
was full of sorrow.

'I don't fear you,' Bran said, bolder now as if he was full of the power of sunlight and it steamed out of him in all directions. And as he grew stronger, Danu seemed to flicker, to diminish in size where she stood.

He moved closer to her. A gust of wind took her hair and it flew across her face. By now he was looming over her and it felt so good.

A rush of awful joy, such as he felt when a deer fell under his arrow pulsed through him. He seized Danu's hair and pulled her head back exposing her throat.

'This is for my brothers,' he said, and leaned down and kissed her neck.

'You are my love,' she said.

'You're so weak,' he told her, 'I could break you like a stick across my thigh.'

Then he plunged the knife up under her ribs and into the heart of the goddess. Instantly she vanished. He could still hear her voice though. She said:

'You are me. You cannot kill me brother. I am you.'

He was left with nothing in his hands but his brother's knife. He threw back his head and laughed to the sky gods and the piercing, roaring, bestial sound he made shook the High Rock.

Yes, it was time for a change.

He climbed down the rock face eager to meet his brother and their friends. He must tell them the truth he'd discovered at the turn of the sun that day.

'The goddess is dead,' he shouted, sweat pouring into his eyes in his exaltation, 'the king does not have to die.'

Voices drifted up to him but he was too high to hear the words. He sensed there was dissent below, heard it in the tones of unrest in the voices of the men.

As he grew closer to the ground he could make out some of the comments.

'Coward,' one man shouted, 'why don't you jump?'

'We are ready for your blood,' shouted another, 'not the sight of your arse.'

'Quickly brother,' this, the voice of Eavan, 'our blood-lust is rising. Will you deny us your sacrifice?'

Bran tried to explain everything as he carried on climbing down, gripping the clefts in the rock, finding each foothold in the swift manner of a champion.

'The king is king of all,' he yelled over his shoulder, 'we are all there is. The queen of earth is an illusion. The goddess is dead. She does not exist. All there is with power - is us. Men.'

When he was near enough to the ground he leaped from the rock face and sprang upright just in time to receive the first

blow across his head. He fell to his
knees, still shouting the good news,
babbling like a madman about his triumph
over the old ways on the High Rock.

    His brothers rained their fists upon
him. They beat at his head and when he
fell forward, they kicked and stamped on
his body. Finally, with the iron taste
of blood in his mouth, his heart fully
alive with the danger and pain, darkness
enveloped him.

When he awoke he knew by the smell of
sweat, skinned animals and bad food that
he was in the lonely house of his
brother, Eavan. Every part of him ached
and the pain between his thighs was such
agony he begged for his handmaids to
bring him poppy juice and cool water.

    A deep voice seemed to arise out of
the depths of his suffering.

    'The goddess is dead. Long live the
king. From now on, you'll be the one to
fetch juice and water. No one serves
you.'

    'I am still the king,' Bran said
though parched lips, 'we men are all
kings now.'

    'You are not one of us. You've been
punished for your sin according to my new
laws. You denied us the blood-song
brother. We took revenge as was our
due.'

    It was Eavan even though he sounded

like a stranger. And at that moment Bran
remembered how much his younger brother
had envied him his fortune when he was
chosen as the Corn King and consort of
the goddess.

When Bran's wife the beauty, Nessa,
bore twin sons – a blessing that would
tumble down all the generations of his
loins, Eavan would not come to the water
blessing ceremony.

And whenever one of the handmaids of
the goddess became pregnant by Bran,
Eavan would shun her as if she was
poison.

Bran opened his eyes. 'You gave me the
knife. I did exactly what you wanted me
to do.'

'You fool,' Eavan said, 'you should
never take the advice of an enemy.'

Bran sat up. The pallet was sticky
with his blood. He ran his hands down
his stomach to his loins to check the
source of his pain. What he found there
made him cry out in disbelief.

'What have you done to me?' he said,
unable to fathom how his day of victory
had turned to dust and failure.

'Don't you see?' Eavan said, 'you've
shown us the way. You've changed
everything. Your sacrifice will never be
forgotten.'

'My sacrifice? I thought we were
ending that barbarism. I thought that
together you and I were taking control of

our destiny. I thought I was setting men
free. Instead you've cut me brother,
you've hurt me deeply.'

He struggled to sit up, his hand
probing tentatively at the gap where his
genitals used to be.

Eavan stood up and folded his arms in
the fading light. He gave Bran no more
words because from that point onwards,
Bran was considered a lowly handmaid, one
of the tribe of slaves who served the
needs of men.

Never again would he nestle in the
arms of his lover.

Never again would his children
recognise him or the men dance with him
or the first blood of an animal be wiped
across his brow.

Instead he would serve the men.

He would be the one to bring food to
the table and watch the men eat. He
would draw water from the spring and wash
the clothes and care for the babes as
they came.

He would submit to the touch of men
who desired him without mercy, as they
did all the females in this new time.

The goddess is dead.

Long live the king.

"We are the cosmos made conscious and life is the means by which the universe understands itself."

Brian Cox

THE END

Made in the USA
Charleston, SC
29 November 2014